Broken Spokes

Broken Spokes

A Play in Seven Scenes

Willy Conley

The Tactile Mind Press
Minneapolis

The Tactile Mind Press, LLC
PO Box 581667
Minneapolis, MN 55458-1667

Printed in the United States of America

Library of Congress Control Number: 2003101753

ISBN 0-9719248-2-1

First Edition

To my "brother"
Jim Conley
and to all those who have lost brothers

Acknowledgements

Special thanks to Shanny Mow, who turned me onto playwriting. Thanks to Sign-Mime extraordinaire Adrian Blue for allowing me to use his "war story" outline, and for teaching me to cherish Sign-Mime, a dying art form in our Deaf culture.

Playwright's Notes

Ideally, all of the actors should be adept in the art of Sign-Mime,* or be willing to learn to achieve a near-native quality from a Deaf consultant skilled in this art form.

Actors playing JACKSON and REBECCA should create a swirl of movement during scene transitions, not only to move props and do tableaux but to represent the state of WESTON's mind.

In situations where a hearing audience is expected, vocal translations should be provided from offstage.

* Sign-Mime, or Visual Vernacular as it is sometimes known, is a dying American Sign Language (ASL) story-telling form. The storyteller employs cinematic camera techniques (wide shot, medium shot, close-up, bird's-eye-view, slow motion, freeze frame, etc.) by use of ASL and body movement.

Production History

Broken Spokes was originally produced by Jaye Austin-Williams and New York Deaf Theatre as a one-act play off-off Broadway at the Peter Xantho Theatre on West 91st Street in New York City during 18-22 January 1990. It was directed by Elizabeth Wolter with the set designed by Jodi Cooper; the lighting by Jack Fennell;

the music by Deborah Maxwell and Laurellie Jacobs; and the stage manager was Jodi Cooper. The cast, in order of appearance, was as follows:

JACKSON: Jim Tola
WESTON: Michael Schwartz
REBECCA: Carole Addabbo
Voices: Mary Grace Lipski, Michael O. Maher

Scenes from *Broken Spokes* were further developed and showcased by producer Robert J. Kruger during the 1990 American Deaf Drama Festival on 16 May 1990 at Callier Theatre of the Deaf at the University of Texas in Dallas. The director was Kelly Cotten with Margaret Soch as assistant director. The English-Sign Language Translator was K. Buddy Bauer. Set and lighting design was by Robert J. Kruger; lights operated by Beth Bohlcke. The cast was as follows:

JACKSON (signer): Sid Johnson
JACKSON (voice): Scott Pierce
WESTON (signer): Matthew Martinez
WESTON (voice): K. Buddy Bauer
REBECCA (signer): Teresa Clennan Dell
REBECCA (voice): Melinda Hall

Broken Spokes was subsequently produced as a full-length play by Robert J. Kruger at the Callier Theatre of the Deaf, University of Texas in Dallas during 7-29 September 1990. It was directed by David Mahfood; set and lighting by Robert J. Kruger; the costumes by Georgia Ford; the sound by Tristan Wilson; the properties by Peggy Kruger; and the ASL translations by Sandra L. Rouse. The cast was as follows:

JACKSON (signer): Sid Johnson
JACKSON (voice): Steven-Shayle Rhodes
WESTON (signer): Gene Mirus
WESTON (voice): Luke Adams
REBECCA (signer): Alandra L. Benjamin
REBECCA (voice): Ann Gerrity-Glover

Broken Spokes was workshopped and showcased as part of the 8th Annual NeWorks '97 Festival produced by Rick DesRochers, Victoria Marsh, and New Theatre at the Boston Center for the Arts during 23-26 January 1997. The director was Janis Cole. The cast was as follows:

WESTON: Ray Rodgers
JACKSON: Gregory Paris
REBECCA: Sabrina Dennison

Broken Spokes was produced by David Zak and Bailiwick Repertory Theatre in Chicago as part of the Deaf Bailiwick Artists series during 14 October-8 November 1998. The director was David Zak with light designed by Eric Appleton. The stage manager was Lisa M. Waugh; the rehearsal interpreter was James Christopher Simon, and the Sign Mime Coach was Chris Lopez. The cast was as follows:

JACKSON: Aaron Christenson
REBECCA: Jonalee Folerzynski
WESTON: Robert Schleifer
Voices: Patti Leahy and Rob Russo

Special Technical Needs

Haunting percussion sounds should be used throughout

the play for transitions and for underscoring. The sounds should be live with the percussionist in a visually unobtrusive location. Care should be taken in the choice of percussion to ensure that the sounds reach the hearts of Deaf people and yet not be obnoxious to the hearing.

When the phone rings or the doorbell goes off, a light flashes to inform the Deaf characters that someone is trying to reach them.

An old-fashioned one-speed bike with the spokes broken on one of the wheels.

A flesh-colored elastic pressure garment—a burn mask used to treat facial burn wounds.

A pair of ear-level hearing aids.

A Telecommunication Device for the Deaf (TDD).

Broken Spokes

A Play in Seven Scenes

Cast of Characters

WESTON: Deaf, articulate in ASL; doesn't use his voice.

JACKSON: Weston's older and bigger hard-of-hearing brother; signs and voices everything.

REBECCA: Weston's Deaf fiancée; articulate in ASL; doesn't use her voice.

Setting

Time: Present.

Place: WESTON's mind. His memories go back and forth between the past and the present at two locations: 1) an imaginary graveyard where his parents are buried and 2) his parents' home. There should be a set piece in the home that doubles as a grave site; examples would be a couple of throw rugs or an ottoman. WESTON should easily cross between the past and the present to the point that the audience is never sure if he is at an actual graveyard. The set can be simple and realistic with touches of surrealistic elements.

Scene One

A solitary light comes on WESTON standing between a couple of imaginary graves. He has an old bike wheel by his side with some broken spokes.

On another level standing apart in a silhouette are JACKSON and REBECCA frozen in a tableau that will be part of an ongoing Sign-Mime piece that they do later on in the play. We should see a triangle formation of three people with WESTON at the apex.

For each of these tableaux, except where noted, JACKSON wears a flesh-colored elastic pressure garment—a burn mask used to treat facial burn wounds. It covers his entire head with openings at the eyes, nose, and mouth.

Long pause as WESTON looks around self-consciously. His behavior borders on psychosis.

WESTON

Mom... Dad... Most hearing people come to a grave to pray. I see them talk to the ground. What do Deaf people do? Sign to the ground? What if you're up there... sitting in the tree? Or up in the sky? I'll just sign out in the open—hope you can see me... some people bring fake flowers—think they'll last forever... make a grave pretty. I want to leave you something real...

Sets bike wheel down.
This is not pretty. I'm sorry I haven't been back since the day we buried you two. It's been… I've been… I want to talk to you two… about Jackson. He's…
Can't find the words; drifts off.

JACKSON, using slow and repetitive motions, signs an image or two from the Car Accident story that he will do in its entirety in Scene Seven. Examples of images would be passing telephone poles and dividing lines. The audience shouldn't have much of a clue to what JACKSON is doing.
This effect, which applies to JACKSON and REBECCA, should be haunting and hypnotic yet not take away too much from WESTON's lines. Sign choice, repetition, rhythm, and tempo should be explored.

REBECCA remains frozen in her tableau.

WESTON
He's changed… he's really changed… for better or worse… I don't know but Jackson… you two gave me a brother that's… that's…
Looks away, hurt and angry.
ARRRGGGHHH!

End of Scene One

Scene Two

As the light fades out from the last movement of JACKSON's Sign-Mime images, the phone rings in WESTON and JACKSON's childhood home and a signal-light goes on and off in time with the ringing. WESTON, in his mid-teens, is working on an old one-speed bike. Next to him is a bowl of popcorn that he eats from. He hurries to answer the phone, but realizes his hands are filled with bike parts, tools, and grease.

JACKSON races in and beats him to the phone. He quickly hooks up the receiver to the TDD (Telecommunication Device for the Deaf) and types a few words. No response. He picks up the phone and gestures to WESTON to get his hearing aid. WESTON finds it and dangles it in front of him.

JACKSON

Signs and voices on the phone out of habit from handling family calls.

THROW IT!

To the phone.

Wait a minute. My little brother stole my hearing aid.

To WESTON.

Throw it, you faggot, this might be an important call for me.

WESTON spits on the hearing aid and then throws it nice and easy. JACKSON almost throws the telephone at WESTON, but thinks better of it. He wipes off the hearing aid and puts it in.

JACKSON

Buh, buh, buh, testing one, two, three. Shit! Battery's almost dead.

To phone.

OK, I can hear just a little bit. Let me tell you how to talk with me. First, please talk loud and clear. OK? OK? Hello? Hel—lo? Come on, I asked you to hang on. HELLO?

Slams phone down.

ASSHOLE! I'M HARD-OF-HEARING SO GIMME A BREAK, HUH?

Walks away. The phone rings again and both boys jump for it. JACKSON pushes WESTON down.

Heh. Heh. Heh. Gotta be quick, little brother.

To phone.

Hello! Jackson here. Who? Say that again? Mrs. what?

WESTON

Who is it?

JACKSON

Flips him the bird.

Wait, lemme tell ya how to talk to me. First, speak loud and clear. Spell out your name. Use the names of the states in our country, like my name is Jackson, so J as in Jersey, A as in Arkansas, C as in California, K—Kentucky, and so on, got it? Go ahead. Uh, what's that?—Arkansas? Okay—A. That Vermont? Yeah, okay—V. WHOA—missed that one. Again. Oklahoma? Okay—O. Nebraska, got it—that's an easy one. All right—that's N.

Pause.

Is that it?

To himself.

A—V—O—N. You sellin' Avon stuff? Yeah? We don't want any—bitch!

Hangs up.

All that for nuthin'! I hate telephones.

Grabs a handful of popcorn. He makes subtle masturbatory gestures at WESTON and as a result shoots popcorn out of his hand, laughing hard at his own joke.

Hey, what time's Mom and Dad gettin' home?

No *reply.*

Yo—I'm talking to you.

Throws a popcorn.

What time's Mom and Dad gettin' home?

No *reply. Throws another popcorn.*

What're you doing with Dad's bike? Huh?

More popcorn.

Answer me. Dad ask you to do that? He want you to do that or are you brown-nosin' him? Huh? Come on, talk to me.

More popcorn.

Ohhh—you're punishing me! Awww, geez I feel so terrible. What did I do?

Silence.

Hey, come on—what're you doing there?

Gives irritating little slaps to WESTON's face.

WESTON

WATCH. YOU HAVE EYES!

JACKSON

Oooh. He's upset. You do everything Mom and Dad tell you. Make your bed, take out the garbage, do your homework. A good boy scout.

Tweaks WESTON's cheeks.

WESTON

Bug off, bird-brain.

JACKSON

Hohoho—naughty-naughty language.

Pause.

What're doin' that in the living room for?

WESTON

Look out the window. See water? From the sky? It's called rain.

JACKSON slaps hard on the back of WESTON's head.

JACKSON

You got an attitude problem.

WESTON

Pause—a diversion.

Who called?

JACKSON

What? Oh... your girlfriend!

WESTON

Get outta here, I don't have a girlfriend.

JACKSON
If you quit beatin' off maybe you'll get a girlfriend.

WESTON tackles JACKSON and they have a scuffle ending with JACKSON on top, straddling WESTON.

WESTON
GET OFF... GET OFF... GET OFFA ME... MY NOSE... BLEEDING!

JACKSON
Awww. Want me to call an ambulance?

WESTON
You bastard.

JACKSON
Hey—you're a lousy wrestler, know that?

WESTON
YOU'RE A LOUSY BROTHER, KNOW THAT?

JACKSON
Slaps him.
Watch it. Oh—you're not gonna cry, are ya?

WESTON
Get off.

JACKSON
Whaddya say?

WESTON
What?

JACKSON
Want me off? What do ya say?

WESTON
I don't know.

JACKSON
Please?

WESTON
Please.

JACKSON
Please, big brother.

WESTON
Please... big brother.

JACKSON
Good boy.

Gets up and when his back is turned, WESTON gives him an "up-yours" gesture.

So, what's up with this bike?

WESTON
Nothing. Why're you worried about it? You got nothing better to do?

JACKSON
You gonna start that shit again? Huh?

WESTON
Get outta here.

JACKSON
HEY! WHAT'S BUGGIN' YOU?

WESTON
YOU MAKE ME FEEL ASHAMED!

JACKSON
Ooohhh. Shame a what?

WESTON
WHAT? You know!

JACKSON
Oh!

Makes more masturbatory gestures with popcorn.

Pup-pup-pup-uh-uh-uh-aaahhh.

WESTON
YOU-YOU EMBARRASSED ME!

JACKSON
Ah, that's nothing.

WESTON
NOTHING? WHAT IF I TOLD MY FRIENDS ABOUT YOU—YOU...

JACKSON
What if you told your friends about me what? Huh?

Shoots more popcorn out of his hand.

WESTON
Very funny.

JACKSON

What did you say before? What if you told your friends you caught me? Ha—won't bother me none. Maybe they'll learn sumthin'—like you should.

No response.

I just told them that I caught you in your room, so what? I didn't tell them I caught you with a pillow—

WESTON

SHUT UP!

JACKSON

If you're nice to me I won't tell anybody.

WESTON

Be nice to you? What do I gotta do?

JACKSON

Hmmm, lemme see… help me out with my Sign-Mime story.

WESTON

Help with your Sign-Mime story? Now? Can't you see I'm working?

JACKSON

Pup-pup-pup-uh-uh…

WESTON

I hate it when you… What story are you working on?

JACKSON

<u>The War Story</u>.

WESTON

That's Dad's story!

JACKSON

Well, I'm changing it around to make it my story.

WESTON

Let me see.

JACKSON

Like a bad actor, he makes a big deal out of preparing to tell his story. The following is The War Story, a Sign-Mime story of a World War II dogfight. This sequence will be Sign-Mimed as a whole in Scene Five (suggested sequence: 5-7).

1. Battleship on high seas.
2. A fat captain on deck scans the horizon with binoculars.
3. A bumble-headed sailor stands at attention next to the captain.
4. Off in the distance, enemy warplanes are approaching.
5. Captain spots them and hands the glasses to the sailor for reassurance.
6. Pilots with goggles and scarves can be seen in the cockpit.
7. One of the pilots signals to another and points down to the ship. He gives a thumbs-up signal and does a nose dive.
8. Captain alerts all of his men to get on deck behind weapons.
9. Pilot lines up his target.
10. Sailors load cannons.

11. Pilot drops a bomb.
12. Captain gapes as the bomb descends towards the boat.
13. He shouts to crew members to fire.
14. The bomb blows up the ship.
15. Pilot looks back and watches the explosion.
16. Pilot scratches in another win on the side of his plane.
17. Smoke clears at the explosion site.
18. The high seas are calm and the planes fly off into the sunset.

WESTON

Whoa, whoa... that's wrong. It's gotta be like a movie. You know they always start with a wide shot of something... first show the battleship like a speck way out in the ocean, and then come in close to the captain on deck.

JACKSON

Bullshit! I'm doing it my way.

WESTON

That's the way Dad taught us.

JACKSON

I'm doing it my way, okay, little brother?

WESTON

You asked me for help.

JACKSON

Just watch!

Does another segment of the story, which is obviously sloppy

and out of sequence (suggested sequence: 12, 6, 10, 8).
How's that?

WESTON
Appeases him with half-hearted hand waves of applause.
Very good.

JACKSON
That better?

WESTON
Oh yeah, much better!

JACKSON
Really? I can't wait to perform this at the Deaf club. People are gonna laugh themselves to tears.

WESTON
Yeah, they'll cry, all right.
Aside.
Cry out of boredom.

JACKSON
What did you say?

WESTON
They're going to cry and laugh. I mean, laugh and cry.

JACKSON
I thought you said boring.

WESTON
Had a booger in my nose.

JACKSON

Pause.

Who taught you how to take that apart?

WESTON

Dad.

JACKSON

He ask you to do that?

WESTON

Yup.

JACKSON

What is that?

WESTON

Brake.

JACKSON

Dad trust you fixin' that brake?

WESTON

Yeah—it's easy.

JACKSON

That bastard. How come he didn't ask me to help him?

WESTON

Maybe you were out.

JACKSON

I wouldn't wanna waste my time on that anyways.

Pause.

He really taught you how to do that?

WESTON

Yeah. So what? All ya gotta do is ask...if you ever get interested in anything.

JACKSON

Fakes a punch.

I bet he sat down and explained it all to you.

WESTON

No. I asked.

JACKSON

Yeah? Like you asked him to show you how to do Sign-Mime stories?

WESTON

Yeah. So?

JACKSON

I asked him to help me.

WESTON

So?

JACKSON

Doesn't Dad give you a little extra help?

WESTON

Sometimes. He knows I want to open a bike shop someday, so he teaches me stuff. You jealous?

JACKSON

No way. If you and Dad are buddy-buddies, fine. I ain't gonna worry about it—okay? Now show me how to put that thing back on.

WESTON demonstrates putting the brake back together. When he gets it together he has JACKSON help put the chain back on. WESTON accidentally turns the pedal wheel, crushing JACKSON's finger between the spikes and the chain.

JACKSON

AAAHHH! STOP IT! STOP. STOP. OH SHIT. OH, MY—

WESTON

Sorry, I'm sorry, I'm sorry—

JACKSON

GIT IT OFF. COME ON—AHHH. Oh man. GEMME SOME ICE.

WESTON

I'm sorry—really.

JACKSON

GO!

WESTON gets ice from the refrigerator.

JACKSON

What you do that for?

WESTON
I said I'm sorry.

JACKSON
Liar! You did that on purpose.

WESTON
Of course not.

JACKSON
Did too—I saw you.

WESTON
It was an accident. I thought your finger was out.

JACKSON
Should have paid more attention.

WESTON
Sorry!

JACKSON
Yeah, sure. Don't worry—just wait and see what I'll tell Mom and Dad.

JACKSON exits. WESTON goes back to the bike wheel. When the lights change, he's at the grave site with a far-away look. JACKSON and REBECCA are in a tableau upstage as in the opening. In slow motion, JACKSON is doing a few vivid and captivating Sign-Mime images and rhythms from the Car Accident story. Long pause.

WESTON
"Just wait and see what I'll tell Mom and Dad"—that's

what he said. And you remember Rebecca?

JACKSON freezes. In slow motion, REBECCA comes out of her tableau and does a few entrancing Sign-Mime images from her Bird and Seed story below, which she will do in its entirety at the close of Scene Six.

REBECCA

1. A bird in flight with a seed in her mouth.
2. Something catches her eye and she drops the seed.
3. The seed falls to the ground, takes root, and begins to grow.
4. Rain and sun turns the seedling into a beautiful flower.
5. Bees fly in to take away pollen.
6. Birds fly in to take away seeds.
7. The flower withers and dries up.
8. Snow falls and kills it.
9. A bird in flight with a seed in her mouth.

End of Scene Two

Scene Three

Morning. WESTON and JACKSON's home. WESTON, in his mid-20s, slowly packs his belongings; he's not very organized or decisive. He comes across the family photo album and takes time to enjoy it. The door light goes on and off intermittently. Quickly, he closes the album, putting it in a box, and collects more things. Piles of stuff are created to give a busy appearance. He opens the door with his arms loaded. REBECCA carries in a large bag and puts it aside.

REBECCA

You took your sweet time.

WESTON

Help! Help!

REBECCA comes over and hugs him, kisses him, nibbles on his ear, etc. Finally, WESTON, no longer able to withstand the torture, drops all of the boxes.

Now I gotta organize this all over again. You're no help.

REBECCA

Maybe I've helped in other ways.

WESTON

Where've you been? Don't give me that dirty look.

REBECCA
Some of us work full-time, sometimes even overtime.

WESTON
I know, I know, it was just an expression, "Where've you been?"

REBECCA
Not everyone receives an inheritance from a rich uncle, gets to set up their own business, be their own boss, keep their own hours—

WESTON
Hey—once I get set up, you may be your own boss.

REBECCA
We will be the boss. One day I order you around, the next day you order me around.

WESTON
Oooh, I like that.
Pause.
Mom and Dad behaving themselves at the retirement community?

REBECCA
They're the best. Never complain. Know the rules. The sweetest couple, the only couple I see that are still very much in love with each other.

WESTON
What's wrong with the other Deaf people there?

REBECCA

They call me for help every hour to find their false teeth... or their eyeglasses, read what the TV guide says or the telephone book.

WESTON

No way! Deaf senior citizens do all that?

REBECCA

Weston, open your eyes. They're the same as hearing senior citizens. How come you've got all those pots and pans and books all together in one box?

WESTON

They uh... go together. Those are cookbooks!

REBECCA

Pulls out Coma and fingerspells.

C-O-M-A. Interesting. I didn't know Robin Cook wrote cookbooks.

WESTON

I meant they're his books—Cook's books.

REBECCA

Very clever. Get out of my way, you're wasting time.

WESTON

What's the hurry?

REBECCA throws a pot at him.

HEY—I'm serious. What's the hurry?

REBECCA

Number one: your parents need to have this house

cleaned out by the end of the week to put on the market. Number two:—

WESTON

The bike shop is ready for us to move in.

REBECCA

And nummmbeeer threee?

No response. Throws another pot at him.

WESTON

What, what? I don't know.

REBECCA

The sooner we can…

WESTON

Let's make love right now.

REBECCA

No, no, no. Read my fingers: w-o-r-k first, p-l-a-y later.

WESTON

Uh-huh, play first, work later.

REBECCA

Uh-huh, work first, play later.

WESTON

Oh, I get it now, work later, play first.

REBECCA
Picks up Coma.
Would you like me to put you in a coma?

WESTON
My knees are knocking.

REBECCA throws Coma at him. He starts to "stalk" her.

REBECCA
Picks up a chair.
Back off, tiger boy.

WESTON
What's in that bag?

REBECCA
Stay out of there. It's my social work reports and stuff I have to write up.

WESTON
Funny-shaped bag for reports. YAHOOO!

REBECCA
What are you all excited about?

WESTON
You finished it?

REBECCA
I don't know what you're talking about.

WESTON

You finished the sign for the bike shop.

REBECCA

No. That's a long way off. It's just paperwork.

WESTON

ALL RIGHT! You finished the sign.

REBECCA

What sign—

WESTON

Gives her a long wet smooch.

Can I open it now?

REBECCA

You're...

WESTON tears open the beautiful gift wrap that obviously took a lot of time and care. A sign is revealed that reads: WEST-BOUND BIKES.

WESTON

Oh, wow! The first Deaf bike shop in America.

REBECCA

Hey, you threw away the little tiny bike I put on the ribbon.

WESTON

Oh sorry. Rebecca, this is perfect. Really—beautiful design. Did you do all of this?

REBECCA
Most of it... your father helped me some with the cutting and letter-carving.

WESTON
Dad helped?

REBECCA
Oh, yeah, they've got a woodshop at the retirement community, remember? Maybe if you visit once in a while, you'll notice.

WESTON
Hey, don't start that. You know I'm trying to get this place cleaned out as fast as I can.

REBECCA
Not fast enough. Move it.

WESTON
It's not easy leaving this place. Spent all my life here.

REBECCA
Well, get over it, grow up, and move on.

WESTON
You're cold.

REBECCA
Fine, do you want more time here? I'll come back next week.

WESTON
Are you getting angry?

REBECCA

Impatient.

WESTON

That's you... ooohhh, and what's in this little bag?

REBECCA snatches it away.

C'mon, what is it?

REBECCA

Pack, tiger.

WESTON

Something else for the bike shop?

REBECCA shakes her head.

Something for our new apartment?

REBECCA shakes her head.

Something for after we get married?

Growls and takes a swipe at her, trying to maul her in an affectionate way.

JACKSON walks in and casually helps himself to a can of Coke from the refrigerator. He watches.

REBECCA

Something we will work in—in our bike shop.

WESTON

Gloves!

REBECCA pulls out two cycle caps and puts them on WESTON and herself. He hugs and kisses her.

WESTON
Sees JACKSON.
Aaahhh!

JACKSON
Hey, West. Working hard?

WESTON
What're you doing here?

JACKSON
I live here, remember?

WESTON
Not any more. What's the matter with your new apartment?

JACKSON
What's up, Bec? You're lookin' good.

WESTON
Did you put up that bookshelf for Mom and Dad yet?

JACKSON
Did I come at a bad time?

REBECCA
What's it look like?

JACKSON
Looks like a good time to me. Except most people take their clothes off. I remember you used to do that pretty good, Bec.

WESTON
What are you talking about?
No response.
Rebecca, what's he talking about?

REBECCA
Oh, he just has diarrhea of the mouth.

JACKSON
Oho, good one, Bec-babe, good one. Don't forget our…
About to say something obscene but instead uses facial expressions and gestures something obscene in an obscure way.

WESTON
What's going on here?

JACKSON
Hey—I just came over to check up on how your move's coming along. I see you move pretty quick, hahaha. She slowin' you down?

WESTON
We're taking a break, all right? Thanks for helping out.

JACKSON
Hey, I already did my share.

WESTON
Yeah, you moved out your clothes.

JACKSON
Wow, where did this sign come from?

WESTON

Kisses REBECCA.

My fiancée made it.

JACKSON

A social worker? Impossible, they don't know what to do with their hands.

REBECCA

I sure—

WESTON

Jack, why're you here?

REBECCA

What skills do you have, you dumb turkey?

Combines the sign "dumb" with the graphic sign for "turkey"—"dumb" handshape goes against the palm of a "five" handshape.

JACKSON

You've—ahem—forgotten my skills?

WESTON

THAT'S ENOUGH! I thought you two made peace when the family decided to move out.

JACKSON

I was out for a quiet walk and got thirsty and stopped by. You don't mind, do you?

REBECCA

Yeah, we do!

JACKSON
What's the boss upset about?

WESTON
Nothing.

REBECCA
Me, boss?

WESTON
Rebecca, take it easy.

REBECCA
Just to make sure there's no misunderstanding—when we move into the bike shop, it'll be off limits to you.

JACKSON
Owww! What if I brought in an old bike that needs restoring?

WESTON
You don't have an old bike.

JACKSON
Dad does. He might give it to me when he gets too old and crippled.

REBECCA
Old and crippled? You're really optimistic about your father, aren't you?

JACKSON
Fact of life... Boss.

REBECCA

Anyway, our shop is not going to be a place for you to hang out, nose around, and drink Coke. It's going to be a professional operation. We'll be very, very busy.

JACKSON

Professional?

Snickers.

WESTON

Come on, Rebecca, cool it. Just ignore him.

To JACKSON, politely.

Stay out of the way, OK?

JACKSON

Sure. I'll supervise.

Silence as they go back to packing while JACKSON wanders around the house. He ends up in front of the full-length window with the deep sill, his back facing WESTON and REBECCA. He takes out a vial of cocaine and snorts a fingernail-ful. WESTON notices him lingering at the window.

WESTON

Do you want something?

JACKSON

Getting chummy.

Nah. Just having one last look from the inside out. We're gonna miss these windows when we move outta here.

WESTON

We? Those old, ugly windows?

JACKSON

They don't make 'em like that anymore. Big, low, can sit inside with your whole body sideways—great view of the neighborhood.

WESTON

Yeah. A great view of dirty sidewalks, busted windows, empty lots. And that lovely graffiti art.

JACKSON

Remember when we were younger and I was making up Sign-Mime stories in the window?

Does a little Sign-Mime.

Hearing people walking by stopped and stared at me thinking I was some circus sideshow freak.

Pause.

Hey—you comin' tonight?

WESTON

Coming where?

JACKSON

The Deaf club!

WESTON

Oh—not tonight.

REBECCA waves for WESTON's attention.

JACKSON

The boss wants you.

REBECCA
Shut up. Do you want to separate these?

WESTON
Please. Put the photo album over there with the magazines.

REBECCA looks through the album.

JACKSON
Guess I'll have to drive Mom and Dad to the club again tonight.

WESTON
Whad'ya mean, again?

JACKSON
Guess I gotta drive them again.

WESTON
Well, last week I was cleaning up your shit in here. You ought to help some by driving.

JACKSON
We should take turns.

WESTON
Get outta here. You've got nothing better to do.

JACKSON
I'm gonna be performin' tonight.

WESTON
You?

REBECCA

Responding with laughter at the album.

Weston, you look sooo cute in this picture... such blonde hair! Small head, big ears. What're you doing in this picture—raking leaves?

WESTON

Oh, please... don't start digging up my childhood. Pack that away.

JACKSON

I signed up for ASL Storytelling Night.

WESTON

Good for you.

JACKSON

I'm really nervous, man. I've been staying up late practicing every night. There's gonna be an award for a hundred dollars plus an article with the winner's picture in the Silent News.

WESTON

What story will you do?

JACKSON

The War Story.

WESTON

Again? They've seen that already. Everybody knows Dad created that.

JACKSON

Yeah, but I'm changing it around some. This one'll be

much better.

WESTON
Good luck.

REBECCA
Responds loudly again to the album.
Verrry interesting birthday picture of you, Jackson. You signed "I-love-you" to the camera. What a shame you couldn't stay as sweet and innocent as that.

JACKSON
Blows a kiss.
"I-love-you" babe.
To WESTON.
Can you please drive Mom and Dad to the club tonight? I wanna go home, crash for a while, and then rehearse a little bit just before I have to be there. Please, man, I'm really tired. I don't wanna be stuck at the club too early, standing around nervous and tired. I need to crash for a bit, man.

WESTON
I can't, Jackson. I'm right in the middle of packing.

REBECCA
Weston has to have all his stuff out by—

JACKSON
Look, boss. I'm talking with my brother, okay?

REBECCA
Talking with your brother. That's good. You talk to him as if he was your boot heel that stepped in dog shit.

Silence as REBECCA exits to WESTON's bedroom.

JACKSON

She on the rag today?

No response.

Look, there's gonna be a lot of people showin' up tonight.

No response.

I gotta win!

No response. Picks up the sign.

Come on, just one little favor?

WESTON

Put that down, please.

JACKSON

Mom and Dad have been wonderin' when you're gonna visit them again. They think you're kinda driftin' away.

WESTON

I stop by every week. Put the sign down.

JACKSON

Not last week.

WESTON

I missed last week—so what? I'm busy doing everybody's shitwork around here. Now, give it to me.

JACKSON

"Busy." Your favorite excuse.

WESTON

You're jealous 'cause you've got no interests except to get your picture in the Silent News.

JACKSON

Bullshit.

WESTON

Will you give me that? That took a lot of time, energy, and-and... love to make.

JACKSON

How do you know? Maybe Rebecca gave the wood-worker a blowjob for it.

WESTON picks up Coma and gets ready to throw it at JACKSON. JACKSON is ready to toss the sign away. REBECCA enters.

WESTON

GET OUT! GO ON—I SAID GET OUT! I mean it.

JACKSON

I'm leavin', I'm leavin'. Don't worry, I'm on my way. I'm leavin'. I'll tell Mom and Dad you don't wanna see them again. Wish me luck tonight.

REBECCA

Watch where you step... big brother.

JACKSON exits. REBECCA slams the door after him and locks it. Lights go down and WESTON is back at the grave site in deep thought. REBECCA and JACKSON go to their usual positions. She continues her Sign-Mime movements from ***Bird and Seed*** *while JACKSON is frozen in a tableau.*

WESTON

"Watch where you step, big brother." That Rebecca, she's tough. Tougher than me.

REBECCA freezes into a tableau. JACKSON breaks out of his and does a different Sign-Mime rhythm and movement from the *Car Accident* *sequence.*

WESTON

Six months. I can't imagine how six months passed... like *(with some gestures)* turning a page in a newspaper. I only wish I could turn the page back.

Lights down.

End of Scene Three

Scene Four

An early autumn morning. WESTON and JACKSON's home six months later. It looks run-down with some of the boxes and furniture still around from Scene Three. JACKSON now has close-cropped hair with a chewed look. His speech and signs are sluggish from head trauma. He is lying on his back on the sofa bed in the living room. The Sunday comics are over his head, and the rest of the newspapers are strewn about the floor along with the dried leaves that have blown in through the window during the night.

JACKSON vaguely signs some images from the end of Scene Three. He screams out loud and hits his face, still covered with the comics. He relaxes and lies down again, not showing his face. Using the sign for airplane, he "flies" his hands over his head.

WESTON enters from his bedroom. Half asleep, he goes to the refrigerator to get some orange juice. He notices the opened refrigerator and disarranged furniture.

Exasperated, he looks around at the mess, not ready to set things right after a number of times. He pours himself a glass of orange juice and sits at the window. The juice is spoiled and he chucks it out the window. By routine, he begins to put things where they belong.

WESTON

Notices the overturned bike. The spokes have broken on one of the wheels.

No!…

WESTON takes the wheel off and examines it. He tries to mend the spokes but some are beyond repair. REBECCA enters with a small bouquet of flowers. She had tried the doorlight but the floor lamp was overturned. She sneaks in and surprises him. He sets the wheel against the sofa bed.

REBECCA

Hello! How are you?

No reply.

You don't look well.

WESTON

In a daze.

He did it again.

REBECCA

Let me start again. Hello!

WESTON

Woke up and found this mess. Jackson had one of his outbursts last night or early this morning. He must've—

REBECCA

Wait—hello! Good morning? I haven't seen you for two weeks. Is that any way to greet me?

WESTON

Coming out of it.

Oh. I'm sorry. Hi.

REBECCA

You're teasing me?

No response.

Come on.

No response.

You're not playing games, are you?

WESTON

I was up late last night telling Jack some stories to help put him to sleep.

REBECCA

I wished you were up late putting me to sleep last night.

Starts to tickle him.

WESTON

Backing up.

Hey, I'm serious. Please cut it out.

REBECCA "stalks" him around the apartment. She catches him and kisses him passionately, almost to the point of foreplay. JACKSON sits up from his reverie and watches. He becomes turned on and starts to play with himself.

REBECCA

Between kisses.

Oh, I miss your smell... it's been so long.

WESTON
Please… stop…

REBECCA
West… let's…

WESTON
No…

REBECCA
… hmmm… why not?

The wheel rolls away from the sofa bed.

WESTON
'Cause… he's…

REBECCA
Stops.
Jackson is not in your bedroom?

WESTON
Uh-huh… he's right there.

REBECCA
OH!

JACKSON
I-LOVE-YOU.

WESTON grabs JACKSON and takes him to the bathroom. REBECCA regains her composure. She finds something to put the flowers in and sets them on the card table.

WESTON

Enters. During the following exchange they clean up.

Cold shower will take care of him.

REBECCA

He's not wearing his burn mask.

WESTON

Yeah, we took it off a couple days ago. His doctor said he can stop wearing it now. The burns on his face have healed some.

REBECCA

Has he revealed anything about the accident?

Signs "accident" in a traumatic way, like a collision.

WESTON

DON'T SIGN THAT!

REBECCA

I'm sorry—I'm sorry—I'm sorry. What did I do?

WESTON

Don't sign that way.

REBECCA

What way?

WESTON

Pause.

Sign… uh… mishap.

Uses the sign combination of SAD-MISTAKE-HAPPEN.

REBECCA

Copies him.

Mishap.

WESTON

Better.

REBECCA

Weston—the sooner you accept the… mishap, the sooner—

WESTON

Yeah, yeah, I know.

REBECCA

… and get on with our life.

WESTON

I don't need social work now, okay?

REBECCA

You can't…

WESTON

Can't what?

REBECCA

Forget it.

WESTON

Go on.

No reply.

I can't help it. He still doesn't remember.

REBECCA
Your mother and father or the accident—sorry.

WESTON
Everything. I'm stuck with everything—grieving, babysitting, nursing… now I can't get back at him for—

JACKSON
Enters naked and dripping wet.
COLD!

WESTON
Aw, Jack, go put your clothes on. It's not nice to be naked in front of visitors.
Takes JACKSON to the bathroom and soon returns.
I can't get through to him.

REBECCA
Those scars! I-I didn't realize how bad it was.
Pause.
Oh, West. You need help.
No reply.

WESTON picks up the bike wheel.

REBECCA
What's this bike doing here?

WESTON
It was Dad's.

REBECCA
Thinking about trying to open up our bike shop again?

WESTON
I'd really like to, but…

REBECCA
But what's wrong?

WESTON
My inheritance money. Most of it is gone—to pay for two cemetery plots and some of Jack's medical bills that the insurance company wouldn't cover.

REBECCA
I told you before that I'd happy to put up more than my share of the money.

WESTON
No, no. That's okay.

REBECCA
Look—I'm your fiancée. One day we're going to have a joint bank account, so you better get used to the idea of helping each other out. We're partners, right?

JACKSON enters.

WESTON
Hold it, hold it.

REBECCA
Well… how are you?

WESTON
Fixing JACKSON's clothes.
You were so good at putting on your clothes all by your-

self. What happened?

JACKSON
Nothin'. Who dat?

REBECCA
Rebecca. Hi.

WESTON
First, let me straighten out your clothes, then I'll tell you who that is, all right?... That's Rebecca. She was here a couple of weeks ago. Don't you remember?

No *response.*

REBECCA
I brought you peanut butter candy. You ate it right up, remember?

JACKSON
Weston, I'm hungry.

WESTON
Sniffing the air.

Wait a minute. You need a clean shirt.

JACKSON
No.

WESTON
You've worn this for three days now, it stinks. Go take it off and put on a clean shirt.

JACKSON
NO!

WESTON

Come on, you smell like a dead raccoon.

JACKSON

Don't care.

WESTON

Look at me. I'm really tired of going through all of this again. I've got this much patience left. We have a guest and I want you to—

REBECCA

Oh, don't worry about me. I don't mind.

WESTON

Wait, I'm not finished.

To JACKSON.

I want you to go to your drawer, pull out a clean shirt, and put it on. Okay? Takes two minutes—that's all. Now what's so hard about that?

JACKSON

Not dirty.

WESTON

I didn't say it was. I said it stinks. Don't believe me? Rebecca, come here and take a whiff.

REBECCA

No, no, I'm not getting involved.

WESTON

See? She doesn't even want to get near you.

JACKSON

So?

WESTON

You're making me mad.

Pause.

Hey, did you say you were hungry?

JACKSON nods.

I see. Who's gonna make you breakfast?

JACKSON thinks. Points to WESTON.

Oho. We've got a problem here. I'm not making you anything until you change that shirt. I'm telling you for the last time—it really stinks.

JACKSON

NOOO! I-I like stink!

WESTON

All right, all right. Don't get upset now, easy, easy... easy. Calm down. I just won't get too close, that's all. What do you want to eat?

JACKSON

Pause.

O's with Coke.

REBECCA laughs.

WESTON

No. No Coke. You need to learn to drink milk. Rebecca, please.

REBECCA

Sorry.

JACKSON
I want O's with Coke.

WESTON
No. It's not good for you.

JACKSON flips the card table.

WESTON
HEY! Calm down.

JACKSON
I WANT O's WITH COKE!

WESTON
Whoa! Take it easy. Take it easy now. Sit. Sit down. I'll get you your Coke. Sit down.

WESTON brings out a Coke. He sets the table, and REBECCA gathers her spilt flowers and refills a cup with water. WESTON grabs a kitchen towel and stuffs it part-way down JACKSON's shirt as a bib.

JACKSON is having trouble with the Coke can. He slaps the table and holds the can out to WESTON.

WESTON
What do you say?
No response.
What—do—you—say?

JACKSON
Please?

REBECCA
Why's he using a fork?

WESTON
He likes to eat his Cheerios with a fork.

REBECCA
What does that do?

WESTON
I don't know. He just likes to strain the Coke and eat all of the O's first. Maybe the cereal leaves a malt flavor, I don't know. Jack, you've known Rebecca for a long time. Are you sure you don't remember her?

JACKSON shrugs his shoulders.

She's my fiancée.

Signs fiancée like a diamond chunk on the ring finger.

We became engaged before the... before you got hurt.

JACKSON

Pointing to REBECCA's ring.

What's that?

WESTON
What?

JACKSON

Mixes up cookie sign with sign for "diamond chunk."

Co-co-cookie.

WESTON
No, no, no—not cookie. Watch me.

Flips JACKSON's palm over and signs "diamond chunk" on the ring finger.

Fiancée.

REBECCA

I'm the woman Weston plans to marry.

JACKSON

Huh?

REBECCA

Look at the ring he gave me. This makes me his fiancée.

JACKSON

Wow. Weston, I want ring. I want that.

Pause.

Why you laugh?

WESTON

It's impossible for us to get married. I'm your brother.

JACKSON

Yeah.

Pause.

I want funny paper.

WESTON

Please.

JACKSON

Please?

WESTON

Yes sir!

Salutes and retrieves comics, stepping over or around the

bike that's in the way.

REBECCA
So what are you going to do with your father's bike?

WESTON
Take it to my shop to restore it a bit.

REBECCA
Your shop?

WESTON
Sorry, I meant ours.

REBECCA
I thought you were out of money.

WESTON
I am, but I've got a little bit of paint and oil left somewhere in a box—enough to fix this bike up. The tools are still there. Thought I'd start slow and try to get my mind focused on restoring old bikes again.

REBECCA
What about Jackson?

WESTON
I'll bring him along. He's got to start getting used to going outside.

REBECCA
He still won't go outside?

WESTON

No. Still gets a tantrum every time I try to take him out.

Pause.

Weird.

REBECCA

What?

WESTON

Since I've moved Jackson here from the hospital, I've never seen him touch Dad's bike. It was never in the way—just leaning against the wall over there.

REBECCA

He probably had a nightmare last night.

WESTON

You know when he was thirteen, he ran away from home one morning on that bike.

REBECCA

Ran away? Really?

WESTON

He got upset because Dad was spending a lot of time coaching me on Sign-Mime.

REBECCA

I can see why he became ups—

JACKSON

Please, I want peanut butter sandwich.

WESTON
Okay, coming up.

REBECCA
You're more fluent and natural at Sign-Mime than he is.

WESTON
Careful—he might understand what you're saying.

REBECCA
He's not watching now.

WESTON
Jack could've asked Dad to help coach him.

REBECCA
Some people have it and some don't.

WESTON
Well, anyway, later that night Jackson came back with one of the wheels bent pretty bad. Told Dad he fell on a curb. Of course, Dad forgave him, went out and bought a new wheel. And know what's ironic? That wheel with the broken spokes there—that was the new wheel Dad bought. Life's funny.

REBECCA
Why? You've got to understand it was natural for him to be upset.

WESTON
What are you on his side for? I knew he purposely rammed that bike into something.

REBECCA

How?

WESTON

There were no scratches on him; no grass stains or dirt; his pants were fine. What would you think?

REBECCA

Well, that is kind of suspicious.

WESTON

The next day at school when I saw him in the hallway, he had this smirk on his face—as if boasting that he had outsmarted my parents again. I know that look well.

JACKSON suddenly screams with a fork stuck to the roof of his mouth.

REBECCA

WESTON!

WESTON

Stunned for a few seconds.

HOLD STILL! Hold—still. Get your hands off. Keep them down. Down! Don't move. Try to relax. Don't move. Hold it. There. Got it. Okay? Better?

JACKSON nods.

What were you doing?

JACKSON

Eatin'.

WESTON

You don't eat the fork, you know. You're supposed to

take it out.

REBECCA
Are you all right?

JACKSON
SHUDDUP!

WESTON
Hey! That wasn't very nice.

REBECCA
Oh, that's all right. Don't worry about it.

WESTON
What did you say that for?

JACKSON
She talk much-much.

REBECCA
Me?

WESTON
Now apologize... go on—say you're sorry.
JACKSON shakes his head.
Come on, please?

JACKSON
Shakes head vigorously.
I want sandwich.

WESTON
Okay, okay. It's almost ready. Your mouth okay now?

JACKSON
Not hurt.

WESTON
I'm sure glad it doesn't. Let me see your mouth. Open up.

JACKSON
AAAHHH.

WESTON
A little red but it looks fine. Maybe a little peanut butter will soothe it.

JACKSON
West, tell me <u>The War Story</u>.

WESTON
I thought you wanted a sandwich. Make up your mind.

JACKSON
C'mon, planes, please? Ratatatatatatat-uhuhuhuhuh-BOOM!

WESTON
I can't make a sandwich and Sign-Mime at the same time. You're gonna have to wait.

JACKSON
I-Love-You.

WESTON
Yeah. Rebecca, can you bring me the sandwich and

the knife over here please? Rebecca? Yo! Are you all right?

REBECCA

Incredulous.

Yeah, yes, I'm all right. Sandwich?

Brings the sandwich.

WESTON

Jack, want me to cut this in squares or triangles?

JACKSON

Triangle.

WESTON

Cuts sandwich in triangles.

What's the matter—you look so touched by all of this.

REBECCA

He's changed so much. I'm just overwhelmed.

WESTON

Why? You've always hated him. If anything, you're probably happy he's this way now.

REBECCA

I'm a human being, not a sick being.

WESTON

You're not the tiniest bit relieved he's this way? I admit I am.

REBECCA

I am not relieved one bit. I am not happy one bit.

Where is all this coming from?

WESTON

Pause.

You remember the day before my parents… ummm, you know… ummm—

REBECCA

Passed away?

WESTON

Nods.

You were over here trying to help me pack. Jackson made some side comments like seeing you with your clothes off… like you two were romantically familiar with each other or something.

REBECCA

Huh?!? What does that got to do with you asking me if I'm happy Jackson's this way?

WESTON

I'm just curious why you're so friendly with him now. The flowers, the peanut butter candy, and so on.

REBECCA

It's-it's because I-I-I care about you and—yes, him too.

WESTON

Why? Because you had something going with him in the past?

REBECCA

IS IT AGAINST THE LAW TO CARE ABOUT YOU

TWO WHEN YOUR LIVES ARE FUCKED UP?

No response.

JACKSON taps WESTON on the shoulder.

WESTON

Sit down and wait. Rebecca's talking. Go on, sit down.

REBECCA

You should see what he wants.

WESTON

He needs to learn to wait.

REBECCA

Well, anyway, I'm trying to help get your life back on track so that we can go on with our wedding plans. Forget the past, it's a waste of time. You need to think about the future... about hanging up our bike shop sign, running a business, having a family. Let me help you. Let me in a little here...

JACKSON

Banging on the table.

WES-TON! WES-TON!

WESTON

Cut it out, will you? What's your problem?

JACKSON

More Coke.

WESTON

In a minute.

To REBECCA.

I need to think about the present.

REBECCA

Well, then you should start by getting Jackson into a mental institution.

WESTON

NO WAY!

Pause.

Now maybe, just maybe, months down the road, I'll see about taking him to an independent living center.

REBECCA

What's stopping you now?

WESTON

He's my only family.

REBECCA

He'll still be your family, no matter where you put him.

WESTON

I need him here. I mean, he needs me.

REBECCA

And I need you.

WESTON

Oh, you don't really need me right now, do you?

No response.

Give me some… slack.

REBECCA

Some what?

WESTON

Some time, some room.

JACKSON starts banging a hole in the upstage wall with his head.

WESTON

HEY! STOP IT, STOP IT!

Runs into his bedroom and brings out JACKSON's burn mask and hold it out in front of him.

JACKSON

Horrified.

NO. NO. GET AWAY. DON'T LIKE, DON'T LIKE. AWAY. AWAY.

Lights go down. WESTON is at the grave site. JACKSON, without his burn mask, and REBECCA are going through their usual Tai Chi-like Sign-Mime movements. Their sign choices should be different than the previous scenes.

WESTON

Holding up the burn mask.

"Don't like, don't like. Away. Away." Jackson screamed when I held up his burn mask. Ironic that when he wore it, it didn't bother him. When he had it off and could see it, he got scared. I guess it's a pretty scary mask. What do you think?

Puts the mask on.

"Don't like, don't like. Away. Away." Hahahaha...

You know, that was the only time in my life that I was able to scare him.

End of Scene Four

Scene Five

A minute later. WESTON slowly withdraws the burn mask that he was holding up.

WESTON
Look at me. Are you okay? I promise I won't do it anymore. You must stop banging your head on walls. You understand?

JACKSON
I want white-cold.

WESTON
Do you understand?

JACKSON
Yeah. I want white-cold.

WESTON
I'm sorry, I didn't know your scar was bothering you that much. Hang on, I'll get it for you.
Exits.

REBECCA
What's wrong?

JACKSON
Y is hot.

REBECCA
Why?

JACKSON
Yes. Hot.

REBECCA
I mean, what from?

JACKSON
I don't know.

REBECCA
Do you have a headache?

JACKSON
Fire.

REBECCA
Fire? From where?

JACKSON
Inside.

REBECCA
Inside where?

JACKSON
Points to his forehead.
Won't go away. Can't make fire go away.

REBECCA

Do you know what causes that fire?

JACKSON

Don't know.

REBECCA

Do you think—maybe—that maybe it was from—you know… from the car—

WESTON

Enters.

Here you go.

JACKSON smears cold cream over the scar on his forehead.

Well, what do you say?

JACKSON

Pause.

Please?

Smears cold cream on his shirt from signing the word "please."

WESTON

No. Thank you.

Pause.

Wait, don't say it.

JACKSON

Thank you.

Cold cream smears on his lips.

WESTON

Too late! We've got a clown here. Here, wipe that off.

Pause.

So, what was that all about?

REBECCA

I was just asking why his head was hot and itchy.

WESTON

What did he say?

REBECCA

Something about fire.

WESTON

Don't talk to him about his head!

REBECCA

What's wrong with that?

WESTON

Might confuse him and make things worse.

REBECCA

Sorry. I was just trying to help.

WESTON

Leave that for the psychologist.

JACKSON

West, tell me <u>The War Story</u>.

WESTON

Only if you promise me something.

JACKSON
Okay.

WESTON
I will tell you the story if you promise to behave yourself after I'm finished.

JACKSON
I promise.

WESTON
After I tell you the story, Rebecca and I need to go out for a little walk. Your head okay?

JACKSON
Yeah. I'm big boy.

WESTON
That's my big brother.

REBECCA
I guess so.

WESTON
Ready for the story?

JACKSON
Yeah!

Weston, using his personal sound effects, begins The War Story. This should be done with comedy. He does sequence 1-4.

JACKSON

Realizes he can't hear the sound effects.

Wait!

REBECCA

What's the matter?

JACKSON

My ears.

WESTON

Oh, I'll get them.

Catches himself.

No, I'm tired of running around. You go get them.

JACKSON

Where?

WESTON

I don't know. Go look.

JACKSON

How?

WESTON

Think. Where did you last leave them?

JACKSON

I don't know.

WESTON

Well, why don't you start with your dresser?

JACKSON exits.

REBECCA
Why is he so obsessed with The War Story?

WESTON
Dad used to tell us that story to cheer us up when we were young.

REBECCA
A story about war to make you guys happy?

WESTON
No, it's not a violent story. It's pretty funny. It's how we started learning Sign-Mime.

REBECCA
How did he do?

WESTON
What do you mean?

REBECCA
You two learned Sign-Mime from that story—so how did Jackson do? I've never really seen him perform. Did he catch on well?

WESTON
Hmm—not really. He understood it clearly but he couldn't grasp the basics. He'd get pissed off at me because I could do it without a lot of struggle.

REBECCA
What did he do?

WESTON

Let's say he was telling a story—I don't know—a story about some beaver cutting down a tree. He would tell it from one viewpoint like—from the beaver's. This is Jackson:

1. Beaver comes to a tree and looks up.
2. Beaver gnaws through the tree.
3. Tree crashes to the ground.

REBECCA

That's it? No!

WESTON

I'm serious. He would do it in a very boring and simple way. If he had asked for help, my father would've showed him something like this:

Quick and informal.

1. Beaver comes up to a tree and looks up at its enormous height. He pats the trunk with his tail.
2. Disturbed, the tree looks down at what's bothering it.
3. Beaver bares his teeth and starts himself up like a chainsaw.
4. Tree shakes its trunk trying to knock off the pest.
5. Beaver gnaws through the trunk.
6. Tree begins to feel dizzy.
7. Beaver whistles for clearance as the tree falls.
8. Tree sees the ground approaching fast.
9. Tree lands in a mud puddle.
10. Beaver puts his foot on the tree and starts flossing his teeth.

REBECCA

Laughs.

You never showed me that one before.

WESTON

That's cuz I just made it up.

REBECCA

Let me try it.

Does a few Sign-Mime moves, either copying WESTON or inventing her own version.

WESTON

That's good. Just like Dad... he throws in a little humor, shows wide shots, medium shots, close-ups.

REBECCA

Yeah, just like a movie camera.

WESTON

But Jackson just didn't want to take the time to work hard at developing a story.

REBECCA

Interesting... now he's asking <u>you</u> to tell him a story. He's not holding any grudges against you.

JACKSON

Enters.

Buh. Buh. Not work. Here—listen.

WESTON

I keep telling you, I haven't worn them since I was five. They're useless for me. You probably have a dead battery. I'll see if I can find you one.

Exits.

REBECCA

You really like that story, huh?

JACKSON nods

How come?

JACKSON shrugs.

Do you remember your father telling you that story?

JACKSON has a puzzled expression.

Your father.

JACKSON

Father?

REBECCA

Finds the family photo album from an unpacked box and brings it to JACKSON.

See? That's your father. You did have a father. And you had a mother too.

JACKSON

Mother?

REBECCA

There's your mother. Everyone has a mother and a father. You did—but—they're dead.

Checks to see if WESTON is returning.

Doesn't Weston talk about them?

JACKSON

Dead?

REBECCA

Demonstrates; very gestural.

Your mother and father were killed—in a car accident. They're no longer alive and walking around, or talking—like you and me. Your Mom and Dad are buried in the ground—dead, like being asleep forever.

JACKSON

Don't understand.

WESTON enters.

REBECCA

Shhh!

WESTON

Found two batteries but I'm not sure if they're still alive. Try 'em.

Pause.

What's the matter? You're acting funny.

REBECCA

Nothing. Suddenly feel a little tired.

JACKSON

Buh buh buh—yeah! Ratatatatatat-uhuhuhuhuhuh. yeah.

WESTON

To REBECCA.

Guess I found some live batteries.

JACKSON

You have ears?

REBECCA

No, never had hearing aids. If I had them I still wouldn't be able to hear a bomb go off.

JACKSON

No?

WESTON

Okay, Jack, you ready?

JACKSON

Yeah!

WESTON

Does The War Story.

JACKSON

Awestruck.

Wow! Show me—bombs.

REBECCA waves her hands in applause.

WESTON

Demonstrates bombs exploding.

Okay, big boy. We're off for our walk now.

REBECCA

See you later.

WESTON

We'll be back in a little while. Hey—we're leaving now—okay? Hello?

JACKSON

Preoccupied with the signs from the story.

Yeah!

REBECCA

He remembered you used to wear hearing aids. Isn't that strange?

WESTON

I don't know how he remembers silly details like that.

REBECCA

He's got some kind of selective memory.

They exit. JACKSON continues to play for a few minutes. Then he notices he is alone, and becomes confused with his surroundings.

JACKSON

Father... mother...

Disarranges the furniture again. After a few objects have been knocked over, the lights fade to black.

Lights up on WESTON who's more visibly disturbed at the grave site. JACKSON and REBECCA do their usual Sign-Mimes with different signs.

WESTON

Dad... Mom... Rebecca once said Jackson had some kind of selective memory. Father... mother... selective memory... father... mother... selective memory... mother... father... memory... selective...

Lights go down.

End of Scene Five

Scene Six

WESTON and JACKSON's home, an hour later. Everything is disarranged and JACKSON is nowhere to be seen. WESTON tries to enter but finds the door blocked partway by some furniture. He flicks the apartment lights off and on a few times. Frantic, he searches every inch of the place.

WESTON

Where'd he go? He never leaves here!

REBECCA

Don't worry, we'll find him.

WESTON looks at the very narrow space under the sofa.

REBECCA

Do you really think Jackson could've flattened himself and crawled under there?

WESTON

I'm going to check with the neighbors.

REBECCA

Wait. I'm going to say this once more. When we find him, you should really consider putting him in a mental hospital.

WESTON

NO!

REBECCA

Why?

WESTON

I told you, he's my only family.

Grabs a pad of paper and is about to exit when REBECCA grabs him.

REBECCA

Look. You've got to start thinking about building a new family. With me. Don't turn away—look at me. Think of everything we've shared together... the first time we met. First day of spring, I remember. The Deaf club. I asked for your autograph. You wouldn't give it to me. Didn't think you were famous enough. I thought you were the most beautiful and talented Sign-Mime storyteller I've ever seen. I still think that way. Wait. Don't go yet. Please? You and me camping and canoeing down the river. Remember? Biking to the beach. Going to wine-tasting festivals. Garage sales. Spaghetti dinners at church. Our first kiss on the church parking lot. The first time we made love... in the woods out back here. Do you want to throw all that out the window?

No response.

Are you planning to babysit him the rest of your life?

WESTON exits. She follows him to the door.

REBECCA

Signs to the door.

I want you to take care of me the rest of your life. Get

out of this place. Get our bike shop started. We'll have children in our little two-bedroom apartment above the shop. There you'll have rebuilt your family. What about me? ME?

WESTON

Enters on "ME?" and sees her standing behind the door.

Forgot a pencil.

Absent-mindedly grabs something out of a pencil holder that feels like a pencil—a toothbrush, candy cane, Slim Jim, whatever.

Well, what's your problem?

REBECCA

I'm losing you.

WESTON

I'm here.

Kisses her and exits. Soon he returns and throws the toothbrush or whatever across the room.

Toothbrush.

WESTON finds a pencil and exits once again. REBECCA resets some of the furniture that was knocked over particularly a piece near the window. After the piece of furniture is reset, she straightens up the curtains. She lifts one of the curtains and makes it into a baby's blanket. She begins to imagine holding a baby.

REBECCA

You adorable thing, how did you get to be so beautiful? Huh? Give me a kiss. Awww—you melt my heart. Look at that! Weston, look. She can sign milk now. Do that again for Mommy, please? How about that? Oh, it's so wonderful seeing signs on those tiny little fingers. Look at her eyes, they're—

JACKSON, who has been crouched on the window sill behind the curtains slowly comes out and chokes REBECCA.

WESTON

Enters.

JACKSON! HEY—

Pounces on his brother and pries him off of REBECCA.

REBECCA

AHHH! GET OFF OF ME! GET OFF! YOU UNDERSTAND? WHAT YOU DO THAT FOR? WHAT FOR?

WESTON

Now, you look at me. You could've really hurt her badly. What do you think you were doing?

JACKSON

I'm sorry. I want play.

REBECCA

YOU UGLY MONSTER! YOU WANTED TO KILL ME. YOU'RE NO KID.

WESTON

Calm down, calm down—let's see if we can work this out.

REBECCA

Calm down? You're asking me to calm down. He was

about to KILL ME while you're out scribbling little notes to your neighbors. He's no—

WESTON
Rebecca—

REBECCA
… he's not kid, I'm telling you. He's sly, watch out.

WESTON
Rebecca, he said he was just playing. He likes to rough-house sometimes. Probably testing you to see if you like it.

REBECCA
What did I tell you about that guy? Aren't you going to listen to me?

WESTON
Of course I listen to you.

REBECCA
You don't trust my judgment.

WESTON
Yes, I do.

REBECCA
No, you don't. I have news for you—you've got a BIG problem.

WESTON
Wait a minute.

REBECCA

I'm leaving.

WESTON

Hey, where are you going?

REBECCA

I SAID I'M LEAVING. ARE YOU BLIND? I—AM—LEAVING. BYE.

WESTON

Come on, be reasonable. He didn't really hurt you that much, did he?

REBECCA

No, he just stroked my hair playfully. GET OUT OF MY WAY.

WESTON

I'm sorry, I'm really sorry. Rebecca?

Lights fade to black. When they come back up WESTON is at the grave site again. Only REBECCA is in the usual Sign-Mime position but frozen.

WESTON

I told Rebecca I'm sorry. I'm really sorry. Rebecca?

REBECCA comes out of her tableau and Sign-Mimes <u>Bird and Seed</u> in a haunting and beautiful manner.

WESTON

Rebecca? I'm really, really sorry. Come here, please? Come sit with me and talk with my mother and father.

The ground's not wet.

Lights go down.

End of Scene Six

Scene Seven

Morning. WESTON and JACKSON's home. Six months later. The bike and boxes are gone, except for the wheel with the broken spokes. It should be on stage in an inconspicuous place. Everything has a neater appearance but dreariness still lingers in the place. JACKSON tests his hearing aids before putting them in.

JACKSON

Buh-buh-buh. Yeah. Good morning, sun! Good morning, plant! What do you say to sun?

Takes the plant's leaves and makes it sign "good morning."

Good morning!

Goes over to make his sofa bed. WESTON enters, waking up, and gets some orange juice.

Good morning!

WESTON

Hey.

JACKSON

How's that?

WESTON

Unenthusiastic.

Very good.

JACKSON
Wanna see me put it away?

WESTON
I believe you.

JACKSON
Watch.

WESTON
Very good.

JACKSON
Thank you. What're we gonna do today?

WESTON
Not much. Relax.

JACKSON
What is today?

WESTON
Where's your calendar?

JACKSON
Gets his calendar.
March—21—first—day—spring.

WESTON
You know what today is, don't you?

JACKSON
Ummm—oh, Sunday! Yeah! You, me off work today.

WESTON

That's right. No painting today.

JACKSON

All right. I like painting but don't like scrape-scrape old paint.

WESTON

How come?

JACKSON

I scrape-scrape—makes me feel chilly.

WESTON

Well, no cold chills today.

JACKSON

Yeah.

Pause.

Weston. Can I show you my Sign-Mime?

WESTON

Sure, later. I want to cook some sweet rolls.

JACKSON

Yeah!

WESTON

Why don't you clean some of our paint brushes. Get them ready for tomorrow.

JACKSON

Sure.

The doorlight goes off and both run for it.

WESTON

Sorry, big brother. Maybe next time.

Opens the door to find the Sunday newspaper outside.

JACKSON

FUNNY PAPER!

Does an odd little dance.

Funny paper, funny paper, funny paper, funny paper, funny paper—

WESTON

Uh-huh. Brushes first.

JACKSON

After I read funny paper?

WESTON

No. I'm gonna make us some sweet rolls while you clean some brushes, OK?

JACKSON

Yeah.

Cleans the brushes that have been sitting in a can of turpentine. WESTON relaxes and flips through the paper.

JACKSON

Weston—need newspaper.

WESTON

I said after you clean the brushes.

JACKSON

I don't want spill on floor.

WESTON

Oh, that's right, good thinking! Let's see...

Pulls out a newspaper section.

Here, we don't need the Opinion section.

JACKSON

Thank you.

WESTON goes to the refrigerator and takes out the ready-made sweet rolls. He pops them in the oven to warm up, then sits down to read the paper. JACKSON eyes him once in a while but doesn't say anything.

JACKSON

What's wrong that man?

WESTON

What man?

JACKSON

Man we paint for—down street.

WESTON

He's got CP.

JACKSON

What's that?

WESTON

Born that way. Pay attention to those brushes.

Silence.

JACKSON
What's wrong that man?

WESTON
Nothing. He can't use his arms, that's all. Brushes!
Pause.
Good boy!
Checks the rolls and takes them out.
Hey—OK, you can stop now. How about some milk?

JACKSON
Yeah!

WESTON
Do I have to do all the work around here?

JACKSON
Sorry, I'll git it.
Pours the milk, and then he stuffs a kitchen towel partway down his shirt for a bib.

WESTON
Got a little sloppy with the milk, huh?

JACKSON
Hard to pour.
They eat in silence for a while.
West. How come that peanut butter candy girl not come over anymore?

WESTON

Pause.

Thought I told you a few times already.

JACKSON

I forgit. Tell me again.

WESTON

No, it's a long story and I want to forget about it.

JACKSON

I like long stories.

WESTON

She stopped coming over because you… she thought I didn't love her anymore.

JACKSON

You love her?

No response.

How come she stopped? You love her?

No response.

I like her. She pretty. Smell pretty. Bring pretty things… candy, flower, pizza—

WESTON

You remember all that?

JACKSON

Some, yeah.

WESTON

Six months ago you didn't want her around at all. What's more, you wanted to kill her that one day.

JACKSON

Me?

WESTON

What else do you remember?

JACKSON

I miss her. Nothing pretty happen here. 'Cept sun, plant, funny paper... and sweet roll.

WESTON

What else do you remember?

JACKSON

Oh! Can I show you my Sign-Mime?

WESTON

Later. Do you remember anything more about Rebecca?

JACKSON

Thinks.

Pretty.

WESTON

I don't think Rebecca really understood what we went through. She kept telling me you would never get better—that I should throw you in a mental institution.

JACKSON

What's that?

WESTON

A place where they lock up crazy people and keep them

forever.

JACKSON

Am I crazy people?

WESTON

Pause.

You used to be. When we were younger—before the mishap.

JACKSON

What I do?

WESTON

You did a lot of crazy stuff—but now look at you today. You've come a long way. It's amazing that—

Sniffs the air.

JACKSON

What?

WESTON

You fart?

JACKSON

Sniffs.

I think so.

WESTON

Can't you control that?

JACKSON

Sometimes. If I think hard.

WESTON

You're gonna have to try and think harder to control that. Geez—smells like somebody died under the table.

JACKSON

Sorry.

WESTON

It's all right. I lost my appetite anyway. Eat up and then go dry the brushes and put them away. I'm gonna lie down and read.

Long silence. The door light goes off and on but WESTON doesn't see it because of reading the newspapers over his head. JACKSON quietly goes over to answer the door, thrilled that he's finally beat his brother to the door. It's REBECCA holding a fruit basket. She's stunned that JACKSON is so happy to see her. Both look at each other a long time, and then JACKSON backs away to WESTON.

JACKSON

Weston… pretty girl here.

WESTON

Who?

JACKSON

Peanut butter candy girl.

WESTON

I'm not in the mood to play imaginary games now.

JACKSON
Look! Pretty girl here.

WESTON
Have you been sniffing paint fumes?

JACKSON
Me serious. Look, please?

WESTON and REBECCA's eyes meet. Long pause.

REBECCA
Peace?

WESTON
Oh, of course, of course. Please come in.

JACKSON
Gets excited again.
May I hang your coat?

WESTON
Jack, easy.

REBECCA
Sure, you may take it. Thank you.

JACKSON
You very welcome.
Puts coat away.

REBECCA
Is that Jackson?
WESTON nods.

These are for you two. My peace offering. I apologize for—

WESTON

Oh, no, no, no. Please. You don't need to apologize. I should be the one who—

REBECCA

No, really I should. It took me a long time to finally understand what you two were going through. I should've—

WESTON

That's okay, really. Honest.

JACKSON

That for us?

REBECCA

I brought it for both of you.

JACKSON

See I told you. She bring pretty things.

REBECCA

What's that?

WESTON

Oh, it's just, umm... nothing. Please have a seat.

REBECCA

What's that funny smell? Like paint thinner and... rotten eggs.

WESTON

Smacks JACKSON in the head when she isn't looking.

That's a-a special blend of paint we're mixing... some weatherproofing stuff.

REBECCA

Oh, you're painting now.

JACKSON

Both of us. Houses. Now we painting for man. He have...

Can't think of the word so he gestures mannerisms of a person with CP.

WESTON

It's not important what he has. What's important is he pays us money to live on and puts food on the table.

JACKSON

Yeah, sweet rolls. That's important!

WESTON

So as you see, we've been freelancing, taking paint jobs here and there trying to support each other.

REBECCA

That's great! Your place looks... better.

WESTON

We're movin' up.

JACKSON

Can I show you my Sign-Mime?

WESTON
Jack, Rebecca just got here. We haven't even—

REBECCA
That's okay. I don't mind.

WESTON
We don't want to see the same olllllld The War Story again.

JACKSON
No! This is new story. I been workin' on it.

WESTON
When? I've never seen you.

JACKSON
After we finish paint. You come home for sleep short time. Me practice.

REBECCA
What's it about?

JACKSON
Something I dream a lot.

WESTON
Oooh—pretty girls?

JACKSON
No. Car.

WESTON
You dream about a car a lot?

JACKSON
Yeah. Driving car.

WESTON
Strange.

REBECCA
Looks interesting. Your face has healed very nicely.

JACKSON
Really? Thank you. Will I have pretty girlfriend like you? Someday?

REBECCA
Are you asking me?

WESTON
What kind of question is that, Jack?

JACKSON
A question.

REBECCA
I think you will one day.

WESTON
Yeah, I agree. Maybe one day, you never know. You'll be surprised.

JACKSON
Really? I love surprise.

REBECCA
Weston, have you showed him your family album?

WESTON

Stunned.

I don't think that's the kind of surprise he wants.

JACKSON

Family what? Say again, please?

REBECCA

I said family—

WESTON

Rebecca, I don't think that's a good idea.

REBECCA

What? I thought it'd be nice for him to see—

WESTON

Shhh. Please?

REBECCA

Just thought it'd be a nice surprise to compare what you two looked like when—

WESTON

No, I don't think so.

JACKSON

STOP THAT! Don't like watching back-forth, back-forth, like... like ping, ping-pong.

WESTON

Where've you seen ping-pong?

JACKSON

Let her finish talk, then you talk.

WESTON

Smacks JACKSON.

Hey—I don't like your attitude!

JACKSON

I'm sorry. But I wanna know what you talk about.

WESTON

Okay, um… we were talking about…

Looks to REBECCA for help.

REBECCA

Talking about pictures of you and your family. See what you and Weston looked like when you were small. I think it'll be a nice surprise.

JACKSON

What me look like? I want surprise.

REBECCA

West, where's the photo album?

WESTON brings out the photo album, carrying it as if it contained a bomb. He hands it to REBECCA.

REBECCA

Me?

WESTON nods and sits down on the sofa with JACKSON and REBECCA. She opens the album.

REBECCA
What do you think? Know who that is?

JACKSON
No, who?

REBECCA
Take your time. Look carefully. Look up close.

JACKSON
Who?

REBECCA
That's you! Look, you've got the same nose.

JACKSON
No. Who's that?

WESTON
She's right, that's you!

JACKSON
Can't be.

WESTON
It's true.

JACKSON
Not me. I know what me look like. Can I show you my Sign-Mime?

WESTON
No, no, no—wait, in a few minutes. Rebecca is showing you our pictures.

To REBECCA.
Show him one of me.

REBECCA
Ah! Here's one of Weston. Small head, big ears. Isn't that cute.

JACKSON
That's not West. He got big head, small ears.

WESTON
We grow up, you know? Rebecca, thanks, I'll take this now. Jack, look at this. See? That's your mother—our mother, holding you when you were a baby.

JACKSON
That me? No. I was never small.

WESTON
Yes, you were. Everybody starts small. Now here's Dad—our father. That's you helping him push a lawn mower, the old-fashioned kind. Isn't that great?

JACKSON
Where motor?

WESTON
You just push it and the blades turn from you pushing it.

JACKSON
Where motor?

WESTON

Here's another one of me—raking up the grass. That thing's three times as tall as me there.

JACKSON

How you cut grass without motor?

WESTON

You just push it. Yeah, yeah, I know what to show you.

JACKSON

Out back has motor.

WESTON

Yeah—somebody cuts the grass out back with a motor. Look here, what do you think of this one? Look hard.

JACKSON

Grass will come up soon.

WESTON

This is Mom holding up your birthday cake—says right here "Jackson's 5th"—she made an I-Love-You shape with the candles. Pretty neat, huh?

JACKSON

Copies the I-Love-You sign from the photo.

Yeah. Chocolate cake.

WESTON

I don't know. It's a black and white picture. Yeah, it looks like chocolate.

JACKSON
I love chocolate.

WESTON
Do you remember that?

JACKSON
Pause.
No.

REBECCA
It's got your name on the cake!

WESTON
Who else can it be?

JACKSON
I want see other page.

WESTON
Good, good. This one?

JACKSON
No. Back.

REBECCA
I think he wants the push mower.

WESTON
Flips the pages back.
This?

JACKSON
No.

WESTON

This?

JACKSON

No.

WESTON

This?

JACKSON

Yeah, that! Can you teach me how cut grass?

WESTON

WILL YOU STOP TALKING ABOUT GRASS? I'M SHOWING YOU OUR FAMILY.

Silence.

What about this one? Look—family portrait. All of us sitting on the front steps right out there.

JACKSON

Don't know those people.

WESTON closes the album.

JACKSON

Will you teach me how to cut grass? Please?

WESTON

Pause.

Maybe, when the grass grows.

JACKSON

Great!

WESTON

Now go put those brushes away.

JACKSON

Can I show you my Sign-Mime after?

WESTON

Yeah.

Puts the album away as JACKSON puts the brushes away.

REBECCA

Maybe I should go now. We can talk another time.

WESTON

No, stay. I'm okay. Jackson might feel hurt if you didn't get to watch his story. I'm sure once he finishes, we'll praise him, and I'll get him to take a nap so we can talk and catch up.

REBECCA

Are you sure? You seem shaken.

WESTON

I'm fine, I'm just... disappointed. He doesn't remember.

JACKSON

Ready?

WESTON

Yeah.

JACKSON
Sit down. Like movies.

REBECCA
How about some popcorn?

JACKSON
Yeah, Weston, can we make some?

WESTON
No! I'm ready for the story.

REBECCA
Why not? It'd be fun.

WESTON
I'll tell you some other time. Go ahead, Jack, we're ready.

JACKSON reenacts the entire Car Accident Sign-Mime. Below is a skeletal outline of the story. Take liberty with fleshing out the sequence, including varying the images' rhythms, textures, and viewpoints.

JACKSON
No voicing.

1. He forms the entire shape of his parents' car with details.
2. Helps parents get in the backseat of the car.
3. Behind the car, he sleepily takes out a vial of cocaine and tries to take some out on his finger. He drops the vial and it breaks on the ground.
4. He climbs in behind the wheel and yawns.

5. He fumbles for the ignition key.
6. Starts car.
7. Adjusts rearview mirror.
8. Turns on headlights.
9. Shifts into gear and drives off.
10. From the corner of his eyes, he sees the dotted dividing line on the highway.
11. Speedometer shows increasing speed.
12. An occasional car passes by.
13. Dotted lines passing by again.
14. He yawns.
15. Speedometer at 65 mph position.
16. He rolls down his window.
17. He sees telephone poles passing by from the other corner of his eyes.
18. He dozes off for a few seconds.
19. Wakes up quickly and looks into the mirror. His parents didn't notice.
20. He takes out some chewing gum. Offers some to his parents.
21. Another car passes by.
22. More dotted lines and telephone poles.
23. Speedometer needle moves farther to the right.
24. His eyelids grow heavy.
25. Dotted lines are passing farther away from the car.
26. Telephone poles are coming in closer.
27. He falls asleep.
28. Car veers over the shoulder.
29. He wakes up to see a telephone pole approaching head-on.
30. He brakes hard and silently screams.
31. Pole comes closer.
32. Car skids and parents fly over the front seat.

33. Car hits the pole.
34. Parents go through the windshield.

With voice.
The End! What you think?

WESTON
W-H-A-T?

JACKSON
You like? What about you? You like?

REBECCA
It was very—

WESTON
What was that?

JACKSON
What?

WESTON
What was that picture?
Gestures.

JACKSON
Man let two people in car.

WESTON
What two people?

JACKSON
Old people, I think.

WESTON
And what's this?
Makes little crosses passing by.

JACKSON
Telephone… um—

WESTON
What was that movement?
Gestures.

REBECCA
Weston, why don't you sit down.

WESTON
What was that movement?
Gestures.

JACKSON
Coke.

WESTON
The man was drinking Coke?

JACKSON
No. Trying to sniff coke.

WESTON
Trying to sniff coke?

JACKSON
But he dropped it.

REBECCA

Weston, don't you cool off for a minute. I'll get you a glass of water.

WESTON

I'm fine. I'm trying to understand this story.

To JACKSON.

What happened to this man? He falls asleep and hits a telephone pole, right?

JACKSON

What?

WESTON

HE FELL ASLEEP AND HIT THE TELEPHONE POLE, RIGHT? AM I RIGHT? SAY SOMETHING.

JACKSON

What you mad for?

WESTON

THE TWO PEOPLE IN THE BACK—WHAT HAPPENED? WHAT WAS THAT? THEY GO THROUGH THE WINDSHIELD?

JACKSON

Reviews impact image.

Yeah.

WESTON

Punches JACKSON in the mouth.

YOU DUMB SHIT! WHAT YOU DO THAT FOR? HUH? HUH? WHY? LOOK AT ME, YOU UGLY

FUCKER.

REBECCA

Why did you do that?

JACKSON

W-W-West—

WESTON

SHUT UP, I DON'T CARE IF YOU'RE BLEEDING. LOOK AT ME. I OUGHTA SMASH YOUR HEAD THROUGH THIS WINDOW.

Starts to slap JACKSON around.

LOOK AT ME, LOOK-AT-ME. MY turn to shove you around. I'M THE ONE in control here. UNDERSTAND?

JACKSON falls backwards over a piece of furniture.

REBECCA

Stands in front of JACKSON.

I will not have you abuse him anymore. Stop it! Can't you see he's suffered enough damage?

WESTON

Never.

Pulls her out of the way. He pounces on JACKSON again and begins choking him.

How do you like that, huh? Feel good? I'll do it some more. Better? Want me to do it again?

JACKSON

Squeals like a stuck pig.

No, no—

WESTON
SHUT UP! YOU WANNA PLAY? Don't you look the other way—I'M TALKING TO YOU. YOU WANNA PLAY? COME ON, LET'S PLAY.

JACKSON
MOM, DAD. MOM—

WESTON
Are you calling Mom and Dad?
Laughs.
HEY! I GOT NEWS FOR YOU—they're gone.

JACKSON
MOM, DAD—

WESTON
They're gone, big brother. THEY'RE DEAD. YOU CAN'T CALL THEM BACK. THEY'RE DEAD! CAN'T YOU GET THAT THROUGH THE FUCKING MESS IN YOUR HEAD? GET-DOWN or I'll knock your teeth out. You'll never chew food again. Got it? NOW YOU LOOK AT ME. WHY?

JACKSON
Why you red?

WESTON
SHUT UP AND ANSWER ME.
No reply. Goes to the refrigerator, opens a Coke can, tries to pour Coke up JACKSON's nose.
Here, snort that! WHAT MADE YOU DO IT? AN SWER ME—why?
No response.

Stop acting dumb. You know things—you're not telling me.

No response.

Okay, you asked for it.

Gets out the burn mask and holds it in front of JACKSON.

JACKSON

AAAHHH. NO NO NO. PLEASE—GO AWAY. AWAY.

WESTON

SEE? You can remember. Tell me, what you're scared of, big boy? It's just a little piece of cloth.

Puts the mask on causing JACKSON to shrink back in horror.

Why you don't like this? Remind you of the burns? Make you feel tight? Closed-in? Huh? How did you get the burns? You were out of cocaine. Didn't have enough to go on. Got tired from being up late at night practicing your STUPID Sign-Mime. Got so tired you rammed into a telephone pole! WHOOOSH! AN ACCIDENT. AN ACCIDENT ACCIDENT! AC-accident.

Pause.

Accident. You killed Mom and Dad.

WESTON takes the mask off and throws it at JACKSON. REBECCA rushes over to JACKSON and holds him.

WESTON

Why don't you go ahead and fuck him. You two were meant for each other anyway.

Long silence. Simply.
Why?

JACKSON
Why you hit me?

Long pause as WESTON breaks down. Lights slowly go down except for the solitary light from the opening of the play. WESTON moves into the same place where he stood over his parents' graves. The bike wheel should be there. JACKSON and REBECCA are in their usual places. A little light spills on them as we see them gesture slowly and repetitively a simple movement or segment from their Sign-Mimes.

WESTON
"Crossed the border."
"Why you hit me?" Do you see why you're here? Jackson doesn't know... doesn't know who you are now. How does that make you feel? Huh?
Pause.
Hello? Sun's going down. Can you see me?... Mom? Dad? Have I done the right thing? Have I? Dad? You glad I brought the wheel?
Sticks the wheel into the ground so that it stands upright.
There! A perfect tombstone. Won't have to borrow money to get one made. Mom?
To various places.
Mom? Mom?
Pause; with desperation.
Jackson doesn't even know you now. How's it feel? Can you see me? The sun's down... but there's a little bit of light left. Can you see me? How's it feel?
Laughs and then the laughter trails off as he realizes he's

all by himself.

The End